Essential Air Fryer Cookbook for Smart People on a Budget

A Collection of Effortless Air Fryer Recipes for Beginners and Advanced Users

TASHA MANN

TABLE OF CONTENTS

INTRODUCTION...8

CHAPTER 1 BREAKFAST 10

1. ZUCCHINI AND WALNUT CAKE WITH MAPLE FLAVOR ICING 10
2. MISTO QUENTE...12
3. BRUSCHETTA...14
4. CREAM BUNS WITH STRAWBERRIES 16
5. BLUEBERRY BUNS 18
6. CAULIFLOWER POTATO MASH...20
7. FRENCH TOAST IN STICKS 21

CHAPTER 2 MAINS 24

8. RICE AND BEAN–STUFFED BELL PEPPERS 24
9. STUFFED PORTABELLA MUSHROOMS 27
10. AVOCADO VEGGIE BURRITOS 30
11. ROASTED SQUASH GORGONZOLA PIZZA 33
12. DELICIOUS BEEF SIRLOIN ROAST 35

CHAPTER 3 SIDES 38

13. EASY GRILLED CORN ON THE COB WITH CILANTRO 38
14. SWEET GRILLED GREEN BEANS 40
15. ROASTED GARDEN VEGGIES..41
16. SUMMERTIME BALSAMIC ROASTED VEGETABLES 43
17. CAULIFLOWER AND CHICKPEA TACOS.................................45

18.   PERFECT AIR FRYER SALMON 47

19.   AIR FRYER BUFFALO CAULIFLOWER 49

20.   AIR FRYER MEXICAN-STYLE STUFFED CHICKEN BREAST 51

CHAPTER 4 FISH AND SEAFOOD 54

21.   RED CURRY SALMON WITH VEGETABLES 54

22.   FISH & CHIPS 56

23.   CREAMY AIR FRYER SALMON 59

24.   AIR-FRIED COD STICKS 60

CHAPTER 5 POULTRY 62

25.   FRUITY CHICKEN BREASTS WITH BBQ SAUCE 62

26.   SAVORY HONEY & GARLIC CHICKEN 64

27.   FAIRE-WORTHY TURKEY LEGS 65

CHAPTER 6 MEAT 68

28.   CHEESY GROUND BEEF 'N MAC TACO CASSEROLE 68

29.   CHEESY HERBS BURGER PATTIES 70

30.   CHEESY POTATO CASSEROLE THE AMISH WAY 72

31.   CHEESY SAUSAGE 'N GRITS BAKE FROM DOWN SOUTH 74

32.   BEEF RECIPE TEXAS-RODEO STYLE 76

CHAPTER 7 VEGETABLES 78

33.   BAKED GARLIC PARSLEY POTATOES 78

34.   ROASTED VEGETABLES 80

35.   BROCCOLI SALAD 81

36. BRUSSELS SPROUTS AND TOMATOES MIX.................................82

37. SPICY CHICKPEAS..83

CHAPTER 8 SOUP AND STEWS 86

38. NOODLE SOUP WITH TOFU..86

CHAPTER 9 SNACKS 88

39. AIR FRYER DARK CHOCOLATE GANACHE 88

40. AIR FRYER BRITISH VICTORIA SPONGE 90

41. SRIRACHA BROCCOLI...92

42. CHEDDAR CHEESE SLICED CAULIFLOWER...................................94

43. CAULIFLOWER HEAD 96

CHAPTER 10 DESSERTS.. 98

44. CREAM CHEESE MUFFINS..98

45. CINNAMON APPLE CHIPS 100

46. CHOCO MUG CAKE 101

47. ALMOND BARS...102

48. COCONUT BERRY PUDDING 104

49. COFFEE COOKIES 105

50. MARBLE CHEESECAKE 107

CONCLUSION 110

Introduction

With technology giving birth to different and unique inventions every day to satisfy the hunger for innovation in society, the everyday kitchen's modernization is also seen. Among the many devices that have made life more comfortable with their usefulness and design, the Air Fryer is an excellent tool with many benefits.

An Air Fryer is a device that cooks food not by using oil but by heated air with no compromise on the dish's texture and flavor. Air Fryer is not only used for frying up food, but can also be used for many other tasks such as grilling, baking, roasting, and many more. It ensures the food is cooked evenly and thoroughly. Its design is such that it fits in a compact area and works via electricity. It has many different parts:

The frying basket: It is a stainless-steel basket in which the food is placed for cooking. It can be replaced by any other utensils, such as a pizza pan. The timer: The timer is set accordingly; a red light indicates when the time has been finished.

The temperature controller: The temperature of the Air Fryer has a high range from 175 to 400F. Adjust the temp knob to achieve the desired temperature.

The air inlet/outlet: It is used to release the hot air and steam that arises during the cooking process from the device's back. It is, therefore, important that the device is always kept in a spacious area.

How to Start Cooking in An Air Fryer?

Firstly, the Air Fryer must be in a spacious place to allow heat to escape and prevent damage to its parts. It should be put on top of a heat resistance surface.

Secondly, pull out the frying basket gently from the machine. It is recommended to preheat the device for 5 minutes before using it. Simply set the desired temperature for 5 mins and then after the time is completed, pull out the basket.

Now place the food inside the container. Not more than 2/3 of the container should be filled. If required, the container can be greased with an oil spray to avoid sticking the food. If fatty foods are placed, add a little bit of water so that the container remains clean.

8

CHAPTER 1

Breakfast

1.   Zucchini and Walnut Cake with Maple Flavor Icing

Preparation Time: 5 minutes

Cooking Time: 35 minutes

Servings: 5

Ingredients:

1 9-ounce package of yellow cake mix

1 egg

⅓ cup of water

½ cup grated zucchini

¼ cup chopped walnuts

¾ tsp. of cinnamon

¼ tsp. nutmeg

¼ tsp. ground ginger

Maple Flavor Glaze

Directions:

Preheat the fryer to a temperature of 350°F. Prepare an 8 x 3⅞ inch loaf pan. Prepare the cake dough according to package directions, using ⅓ cup of water instead of ½ cup. Add zucchini, nuts, cinnamon, nutmeg, and ginger.

Pour the dough into the prepared mold and put it inside the basket. Bake until a toothpick inserted in the middle of the cake is clean when removed for 32 to 34 minutes.

Remove the cake from the fryer and let it cool on a grill for 10 minutes. Then, remove the cake and place it

Nutrition:

Calories 196 Carbohydrates 27g Fat 11g

Protein 1g

2.   Misto Quente

Preparation Time: 5 minutes

Cooking Time: 10 minutes

Servings: 4

Ingredients:

4 slices of bread without shell

4 slices of turkey breast

4 slices of cheese

2 tbsp. cream cheese

2 spoons of butter

Directions:

Preheat the air fryer. Set the timer of 5 minutes and the temperature to 200CUP

Pass the butter on one side of the slice of bread, and on the other side of the slice, the cream cheese. Mount the sandwiches placing two slices of turkey breast and two slices cheese between the breads, with the cream cheese inside and the side with butter.

Place the sandwiches in the basket of the air fryer. Set the timer of the air fryer for 5 minutes and press the power button.

Nutrition:

Calories 340

Fat 15g

Carbohydrates 32g

Protein 15g

3. Bruschetta

Preparation Time: 5 minutes

Cooking Time: 10 minutes

Servings: 2

Ingredients:

4 slices of Italian bread

1 cup chopped tomato tea

1 cup grated mozzarella tea

Olive oil

Oregano, salt, and pepper

4 fresh basil leaves

Directions:

Preheat the air fryer. Set the timer of 5 minutes and the temperature to 2000CUP

Sprinkle the slices of Italian bread with olive oil. Divide the chopped tomatoes and mozzarella between the slices. Season with salt, pepper, and oregano.

Put oil in the filling. Place a basil leaf on top of each slice.

Put the bruschetta in the basket of the air fryer being careful not to spill the filling. Set the timer of 5 minutes, set the temperature to 180C, and press the power button.

Transfer the bruschetta to a plate and serve.

Nutrition:

Calories 434

Fat 14g

Carbohydrates 63g

Protein 11g

4.   Cream Buns with Strawberries

Preparation Time: 10 minutes

Cooking Time: 12 minutes

Servings: 6

Ingredients:

240g all-purpose flour

50g granulated sugar

8g baking powder

1g of salt

85g chopped cold butter

84g chopped fresh strawberries

120 ml whipping cream

2 large eggs

10 ml vanilla extract 5 ml of water

Directions:

Sift flour, sugar, baking powder and salt in a large bowl. Put

the butter with the flour using a blender or your hands until the mixture resembles thick crumbs. Mix the strawberries in the flour mixture. Set aside for the mixture to stand. Beat the whipping cream, 1 egg and the vanilla extract in a separate bowl.

Put the cream mixture in the flour mixture until they are homogeneous, then spread the mixture to a thickness of 38 mm. Use a round cookie cutter to cut the buns. Spread the buns with a combination of egg and water. Set aside

Preheat the air fryer, set it to 180°CUP Place baking paper in the preheated inner basket. Place the buns on top of the baking paper and cook for 12 minutes at 180°C, until golden brown.

Nutrition:

Calories 150

Fat 14g

Carbohydrates 3g

Protein 11g

5.   Blueberry Buns

Preparation Time: 10 minutes

Cooking Time: 12 minutes

Servings: 6

Ingredients:

240g all-purpose flour

50g granulated sugar

8g baking powder

2g of salt

85g chopped cold butter

85g of fresh blueberries

3g grated fresh ginger

113 ml whipping cream

2 large eggs 4 ml vanilla extract 5 ml of water

Directions:

Put sugar, flour, baking powder and salt in a large bowl. Put

the butter with the flour using a blender or your hands until the mixture resembles thick crumbs. Mix the blueberries and ginger in the flour mixture and set aside

Mix the whipping cream, 1 egg and the vanilla extract in a different container. Put the cream mixture with the flour mixture until combined. Shape the dough until it reaches a thickness of approximately 38 mm and cut it into eighths. Spread the buns with a combination of egg and water. Set aside Preheat the air fryer set it to 180°CUP

Place baking paper in the preheated inner basket and place the buns on top of the paper. Cook for 12 minutes at 180°C, until golden brown

Nutrition:

Calories 105 Fat 1.64g Carbohydrates: 20.09g

Protein 2.43g

6.   Cauliflower Potato Mash

Preparation Time: 20 minutes

Cooking Time: 10 minutes

Servings: 4

Ingredients:

2 cups potatoes, peeled and cubed

2 tbsp. butter

¼ cup milk

10 oz. cauliflower florets

¾ tsp. salt

Directions:

Add water to the saucepan and bring to boil. Reduce heat and simmer for 10 minutes. Drain vegetables well. Transfer vegetables, butter, milk, and salt in a blender and blend until smooth. Serve and enjoy.

Nutrition:

Calories 128 Fat 6.2 g Carbohydrates 16.3 g Protein 3.2 g

7.   French Toast in Sticks

Preparation Time: 5 minutes

Cooking Time: 10 minutes

Servings: 4

Ingredients:

4 slices of white bread, 38 mm thick, preferably hard

2 eggs

60 ml of milk

15 ml maple sauce

2 ml vanilla extract

Nonstick Spray Oil

38g of sugar

3 ground cinnamon

Maple syrup, to serve Sugar to sprinkle

Directions:

Cut each slice of bread into thirds making 12 pieces. Place sideways. Beat the eggs, milk, maple syrup and vanilla. Preheat the air fryer, set it to 175°CUP. Dip the sliced bread in the egg mixture and place it in the preheated air fryer. Sprinkle French toast generously with oil spray.

Cook French toast for 10 minutes at 175°CUP Turn the toast halfway through cooking. Mix the sugar and cinnamon in a bowl. Cover the French toast with the sugar and cinnamon mixture when you have finished cooking. Serve with Maple syrup and sprinkle with powdered sugar

Nutrition:

Calories 128

Fat 6.2 g

Carbohydrates 16.3g

Protein 3.2g

CHAPTER 2

Mains

8.   Rice and Bean–Stuffed Bell Peppers

Preparation Time: 20 minutes

Cooking Time:20 minutes

Servings:4

Ingredients:

4 large red bell peppers

1 (10-ounce) package frozen cooked brown rice, thawed

1 (15-ounce) can black beans, rinsed and drained

1 cup frozen corn kernels, thawed

1 cup shredded Muenster cheese, divided

½ cup salsa

3 scallions, chopped

2 teaspoons chili powder

½ teaspoon ground cumin

½ teaspoon sea salt

¼ cup grated Parmesan cheese

Directions:

Rinse the peppers and dry them. Cut off the tops and discard them. Remove the membranes and seeds, being careful to not pierce the pepper sides or bottom.

In a large bowl, combine the rice, black beans, corn, and ½ cup of Muenster cheese, salsa, scallions, chili powder, cumin, and salt and mix well. Stuff the peppers with this mixture, overstuffing them a bit as the filling will shrink as it cooks.

Put the peppers in the air fryer basket, nestling them against one another so they stay upright.

Set or preheat the air fryer to 350°F. Bake the stuffed peppers for 10 minutes.

Top with the remaining ½ cup of Muenster cheese and the Parmesan cheese and continue baking for 5 to 10 minutes or until the peppers are softened, the filling is hot, and the cheese is melted. Serve.

Nutrition:

Calories 372

Protein 19g

Fat 12g

Saturated Fat 7g

Carbs 52g

Sugar 9g

Sodium 721g

Fiber 10g

9.   Stuffed Portabella Mushrooms

Preparation Time: 15 minutes

Cooking Time:15 minutes Servings:3

Ingredients:

6 (4-inch) portabella mushrooms

2 tablespoons olive oil, divided

1 small onion, chopped

2 garlic cloves, minced

1 cup frozen cut-leaf spinach, thawed and well drained

4 oil-packed sun-dried tomatoes, drained and chopped

½ teaspoon dried thyme

½ teaspoon dried marjoram

¼ teaspoon sea salt

⅛ Teaspoon freshly ground black pepper

⅔ Cup shredded provolone cheese

⅓ cup ricotta cheese

¼ cup grated Parmesan cheese

Directions:

Rinse the mushrooms briefly under cool running water and pat dry. Carefully pull out the stem from each mushroom and discard.

Using a small spoon, gently scrape out the mushroom gills to make more room for the filling. Set aside. In a small saucepan over medium heat, combine 1 tablespoon of the olive oil, the onion, and garlic; cook, stirring often, for about 3 minutes or until crisp-tender.

Place the onion and garlic in a medium bowl and add the spinach, tomatoes, thyme, marjoram, salt, and pepper and toss. Stir in the provolone and ricotta cheeses until combined. Fill the mushroom caps with the spinach mixture and sprinkle with the Parmesan cheese. Brush the edges of the mushrooms with the remaining 1 tablespoon of olive oil. Arrange three mushrooms in the air fryer basket. Place the raised rack on top and add the remaining three stuffed mushrooms.

Set or preheat the air fryer to 350°F. Bake for 10 to 15 minutes or until the mushrooms are tender and the filling is hot. Serve.

Nutrition:

Calories 320 Protein 19g

Fat 22g Saturated Fat 9g

Carbs 15g Sugar 4g

Sodium 564g Fiber 4g

10. Avocado Veggie Burritos

Preparation Time: 15 minutes

Cooking Time:6 minutes, plus 12 minutes to heat if desired

Servings:4

Ingredients:

1 onion, chopped

1 red bell pepper, chopped

1 tablespoon olive oil

3 plum tomatoes, seeded and chopped

1 cup frozen corn kernels, thawed

2 teaspoons chili powder

½ teaspoon sea salt

⅛ Teaspoon freshly ground black pepper

1 avocado, flesh removed

1 tablespoon freshly squeezed lemon juice

4 (8-inch) flour tortillas

1½ cups shredded pepper Jack cheese

Directions:

Combine the onion and red bell pepper in the air fryer basket. Drizzle with the olive oil and toss to coat.

Set or preheat the air fryer to 375°F. Roast 4 to 6 minutes, or until the vegetables are tender. Transfer the vegetables to a medium bowl; let the air fryer basket cool for 10 minutes, then rinse out the basket and dry it.

Put the tomatoes, corn, chili powder, salt, and pepper in the bowl and mix to combine.

In a small bowl, mash the avocado with the lemon juice.

Warm the tortillas according to the package directions.

Put the tortillas on a work surface. Spread each with the avocado mixture and sprinkle with the cheese. Top with the vegetable mixture.

Fold up the bottoms of the tortillas, then fold in the sides and roll up, enclosing the filling.

At this point you can serve the burritos as-is or heat them until they are crisp.

To heat, set or preheat the air fryer to 375°F. Seal the burritos with a toothpick if necessary. Then place the burritos, seam-side down, in the basket; mist with cooking oil. Bake for 5 minutes, then turn over carefully, mist with oil again, and bake for 4 to 7 minutes more until crisp.

Serve.

Nutrition:

Calories 491

Protein 18g

Fat 28g

Saturated Fat 11g

Carbs 46g

11. Roasted Squash Gorgonzola Pizza

Preparation Time: 10 minutes

Cooking Time:42 minutes

Servings:4

Ingredients:

1 (16-ounce) package cubed fresh butternut squash

2 tablespoons olive oil

½ teaspoon sea salt

⅛ Teaspoon freshly ground black pepper

1 (8-ounce) package cream cheese, at room temperature

2 tablespoons sour cream

2 (8-inch) round focaccia breads

⅔ Cup crumbled gorgonzola cheese

Directions:

Place the squash in the air fryer basket, drizzle with the olive

oil, and sprinkle with the salt and pepper. Toss to coat.

Set or preheat the air fryer to 400°F. Roast for 15 to 20 minutes, tossing once halfway through cooking time, until the squash is tender and light brown around the edges.

Transfer to a bowl. Clean the air fryer basket before you start the pizzas.

In a small bowl, combine the cream cheese and sour cream and beat until smooth. Spread this mixture onto the focaccia breads.

Divide the roasted squash and the gorgonzola between the two pizzas. Working in batches, place one pizza in the air fryer basket.

Set or preheat the air fryer to 400°F. Bake for 7 to 11 minutes or until the crust is crisp and the pizza is hot. Repeat with remaining pizza. Serve hot.

Nutrition:

Calories 441 Protein 13g Fat 29g Saturated Fat 15g

Carbs 32g

12. Delicious Beef Sirloin Roast

Preparation Time: 10 minutes

Cooking Time: 50 minutes

Servings: 8

Ingredients:

2½ pounds sirloin roast

Salt and ground black pepper, as required

Directions:

Rub the roast with salt and black pepper generously.

Insert the rotisserie rod through the roast.

Insert the rotisserie forks, one on each side of the rod to secure the rod to the chicken.

Arrange the drip pan in the bottom of Instant Vortex Plus Air Fryer Oven cooking chamber.

Select "Roast" and then adjust the temperature to 350 degrees F.

Set the timer for 50 minutes and press the "Start".

When the display shows "Add Food" press the red lever down and load the left side of the rod into the Vortex.

Now, slide the rod's left side into the groove along the metal bar so it doesn't move.

Then, close the door and touch "Rotate".

When cooking time is complete, press the red lever to release the rod.

Remove from the Vortex and place the roast onto a platter for about 10 minutes before slicing.

With a sharp knife, cut the roast into desired sized slices and serve.

Nutrition: Calories 201

Total Fat 8.8 g Saturated Fat 3.1 g

Cholesterol 94 mg Sodium 88 mg

Protein 28.9 g

CHAPTER 3

Sides

13.   Easy Grilled Corn on the Cob with Cilantro

Preparation Time: 5 minutes Cooking Time: 10 minutes

Servings: 4

Ingredients:

Salt to taste for topping 1 teaspoon fresh lemon zest for topping 4 medium corn cobs, husks removed

Grease for spraying 1 teaspoon sliced fresh cilantro for topping

Directions:

Place the dripping pan at the bottom of the air fryer and preheat the oven at Air Fry mode at 400 F for 2 to 3 minutes.

Lay the corn cobs in the cooking tray, spray with some olive oil on all sides and season with some salt. Move the tray onto the middle rack of the oven and close the oven. Set the timer for 10 minutes and press Start. Cook until the timer reads to the end while turning the corn every 2 minutes. When prepared, transfer to a plate and top with the lemon zest and cilantro. Serve right away.

Nutrition:

Calories 192

Total Fat 4.74 g

Total Carbs 38.96 g

Fiber 4.6 g

Protein 5.43 g

Sugar 0.13 g

Sodium 9mg

14.   Sweet Grilled Green Beans

Preparation: 10 minutes Cooking: 8 minutes Servings: 4

Ingredients:

1 tablespoon honey 1 lb. green beans 1 tablespoon olive oil

Directions:

Place the dripping pan at the bottom of the air fryer and preheat the oven at Air Fry mode at 400 F for 2 to 3 minutes. In a medium bowl, mix the green beans, honey, and olive oil. Put the green beans into the rotisserie basket and near to seal. Connect the rotisserie basket to the lever in the oven and close the door. Set the timer for 8 minutes and press Start. Cook up until golden brown and tender. When ready, move the green beans to serving bowls and serve immediately.

Nutrition:

Calories 81 Total Fat 3.26 g Total Carbs 12.23 g

Fiber 3.1 g Protein 2.09 g Sugar 8.01 g

Sodium 7mg

15.   Roasted Garden Veggies

Preparation Time: 10 minutes

Cooking Time: 12 minutes

Servings: 4

Ingredients:

8 oz. infant bella mushrooms, cleaned up and ends trimmed

12 oz. cherry tomatoes

½ tablespoon dried oregano 1 teaspoon dried thyme

12 oz. baby potatoes, scrubbed and halved (optional).

2 medium zucchinis, cut into 1-inch half-moons.

12 big garlic cloves, peeled.

Olive oil for drizzling. Salt and black pepper to taste.

¼ cup grated Pecorino Romano cheese for garnishing.

¼ teaspoon red chili flakes for topping.

Directions:

Place the leaking pan at the bottom of the air fryer and pre-

heat the oven at Roast mode at 400 F for 2 to 3 minutes. In a big bowl, mix ingredients as much as the cheese and spread out the mixture in a 9-inch baking meal. Slide the cooking tray upside down onto the middle rack of the oven, place the meal on top and close the oven. Set the timer for 10 or 12 minutes, and press Start. Cook until the veggies are tender. Transfer the veggies to a serving platter when all set, garnish with the cheese, red chili flakes, and serve warm.

Nutrition:

Calories 333

Total Fat 2.67 g Total Carbs 76.43 g

Fiber 10.7 g Protein 10.81 g

Sugar 13.5 g Sodium 10mg.

16. Summertime Balsamic Roasted Vegetables

Preparation Time: 10 minutes

Cooking Time: 10 minutes

Servings: 4

Ingredients:

1 small red onion, peeled and cut into wedges.

2 medium zucchinis, cut into 1-inch pieces.

1 teaspoon dried basil.

1 tablespoon balsamic vinegar.

1 red bell pepper, deseeded and cut into 1-inch pieces.

1 yellow squash, cut into 1-inch pieces.

2 tablespoon olive oil.

Salt and black pepper to taste.

¼ cup sliced fresh parsley.

Directions:

Insert the leaking pan at the bottom of the air fryer and preheat the oven at Roast mode at 400 F for 2 to 3 minutes.

In a large bowl, add all the ingredients and spread out the mix in a 9-inch baking dish. Slide the cooking tray upside down onto the middle rack of the oven, place the meal on the top and close the oven. Set the timer for 10 minutes, and press Start. Cook up until the vegetables are tender. Transfer the veggies to a serving platter when prepared and serve warm.

Nutrition:

Calories 82

Total Fat 6.9 g

Total Carbs 4.87 g

Fiber 0.9 g

Protein 0.95 g

Sugar 2.55 g

Sodium 6mg.

17. Cauliflower and Chickpea Tacos

Preparation Time: 15 minutes

Cooking Time:25 minutes

Servings:6

Ingredients:

1 tablespoon olive oil 1 tablespoon lime juice

1 teaspoon chili powder 1 teaspoon ground cumin

1 teaspoon sea salt

¼ teaspoon garlic powder

1 can (15 ounces) canned chickpeas

1 Little head of cauliflower, cut into pieces of bite-size

For the Sauce:

1 cup sour cream

¼ cup freshly chopped coriander

1/8 cup lime juice

1 tablespoon sriracha

Salt to taste

6 (6 inches) corn tortillas

Directions:

Preheat an air fryer to 370 °F (190 °C).

In a large bowl, whisk together olive oil, lime juice, chili powder, cumin, salt, and garlic powder. Add the chickpeas and cauliflower and mix until coated evenly.

Stir sour cream, Cilantro, lime juice, and Sriracha together in a bowl until mixed evenly. Season with salt.

Place cauliflower mixture in the air fryer basket. Cook and shake after 10 minutes, then cook for another 10 minutes. Remove again and cook for about 5 minutes, until desired crispness.

Use a spoon to put the mixture over the corn tortillas and drizzle sauce on the top.

Nutrition:

232 calories 11.8 g total fat 17 mg cholesterol 616 mg sodium 27.6 g carbohydrates 6.1 g protein

18.   Perfect Air Fryer Salmon

Preparation Time: 5 minutes

Cooking Time:7 minutes

Servings:2

Ingredients:

Wild salmon fillets: 2 fillets of similar thickness, 1-1/12-inches thick

Avocado oil or olive oil: 2 teaspoons

Paprika: 2 teaspoons

Salt and black pepper for seasoning

Lemon wedge

Directions:

If possible, remove any bones from your salmon, and allow the fish to sit on the counter for an hour. Season each filet with olive oil and paprika, salt, and pepper.

Place filets in the air fryer basket. Set air-fryer at 390 degrees and air fry for 7 minutes.

When the timer leaves, open the basket and check the filets with a fork to ensure that they are done to your desired doneness.

Nutrition:

Calories 288

Calories from Fat 170

Fat 18.9g

Cholesterol 78mg

Sodium 80.6mg

Potassium 52.5mg

Carbohydrates 1.4g

Fiber 0.8g

Sugar 0.3g

Protein 28.3g

19.   Air Fryer Buffalo Cauliflower

Preparation Time: 5 minutes

Cooking Time:15 minutes

Servings:2

Ingredients:

Cauliflower: ½ head

Red Hot Buffalo Wing Sauce with 1/2 cup buffalo sauce, 120 mL

Olive oil: 2 tablespoon

Garlic powder: 1 teaspoon

Salt: ½ teaspoon

To Servings: creamy dip and celery stalks (like ranch or bleu cheese).

Directions:

Cut the cauliflower into florets of bite-size. Gently stir cauliflower and all remaining ingredients together in a large bowl.

Fill your air fryer basket or rack with light grease. Arrange cauliflower in one layer (working in batches if not all of them suit in one layer). Cook for 12 to 15 minutes at 375 ° F (190 ° C) or until tender and slightly brown.

Serve warm with your favorite celery sticks and dipping sauce.

Nutrition:

Calories 141 Carbs 4.5g

Protein 1.6g Fat 14.1g

Saturated Fat 2g Cholesterol 0mg

20. Air Fryer Mexican-style Stuffed Chicken Breast

Preparation Time: 20 minutes

Cooking Time:10 minutes

Servings:2

Ingredients:

4 inches extra-long toothpicks

4 teaspoons, chili powder, divided

4 teaspoons of ground cumin, divided

1 chicken breast skinless and boneless

2 teaspoons chipotle flakes

2 teaspoons mexican oregano

Salt and ground pepper to taste

1/2 red pepper, cut into thin strips

1/2 onion, cut in thin stripes

1 fresh jalapeno pepper, cut in thin stripes

2 teaspoons corn oil

Juice of 1/2 lime

Directions:

Place the toothpicks in a small bowl and cover with water; let them soak for a while so they won't burn during cooking.

In a shallow dish, mix together 2 teaspoons of chili powder and 2 teaspoons of cumin.

Preheat the air fryer to 400 °F (200 °C).

Place the breast on a flat working surface. Horizontally cut through the middle. Pound up to around 1/4-inch thickness per half using a kitchen mallet or rolling pin.

Sprinkle with remaining chili powder, remaining cumin, chipotle flakes, oregano, salt, and pepper evenly on each breast portion. Fill up the center of 1 half of the breast with 1/2 of the bell pepper, onion, and jalapeno. Roll the chicken upwards from the tapered end and use 2 toothpicks to secure it. Repeat with other breasts, spices, and vegetables and use the remaining toothpicks to secure it. In the shallow bowl, roll each roll-up into the chili-cumin mixture while drizzling with olive oil until coated evenly.

Place roll-ups with the toothpick side facing up, in the air-fryer basket. Set a 6-minute timer.

Turn over roll-ups. Continue cooking in the air fryer until the juices run clear, and an instant-read thermometer reads at least 165 degrees F (74 degrees C) when inserted into the center, about 5 minutes more.

Drizzle the lime juice evenly before serving onto roll-ups.

Nutrition:

Calories 185.3

Protein 14.8g

Carbohydrates 15.2g

Sodium 170.8 mg

CHAPTER 4

Fish and Seafood

21.   Red Curry Salmon With Vegetables

Preparation Time: 10 minutes

Cooking Time: 10 minutes

Servings: 4

Ingredients:

1 tbsp red curry paste

1 tbsp full-fat coconut milk

1 tsp freshly squeezed lime juice

4 oz.salmon fillets

1 lb.asparagus, woody ends trimmed

1 red bell pepper, sliced

celtic sea salt or kosher salt

freshly ground black pepper

Olive oil cooking spray

Directions:

In a small bowl, stir together the curry paste, coconut milk, and lime juice to form a smooth paste. Spread the curry paste over the salmon skin. In your air fryer's basket, combine the asparagus and red bell pepper. Season it with pepper and salt. Spritz the vegetables with cooking spray. Put the salmon, skin-side up, on top of the vegetables. Fry at 375°F for 5 to 8 minutes until the salmon is cooked through and flakes easily with a fork.

Nutrition:

Calories 345 Fat 23

Protein 30g Carbs 9g

22.   Fish & Chips

Preparation Time: 10 minutes

Cooking Time: 10 minutes

Servings: 4

Ingredients:

2 large eggs, lightly beaten

½ cup plain bread crumbs

4 oz.tilapia or haddock fillet

All-purpose flour

Eltic sea salt or kosher salt

Freshly ground black pepper

olive oil cooking spray

2 russet potatoes, cut into ¼-inch planks

1 tbsp extra-virgin olive oil

2 cups coleslaw mix

1 tbsp extra-virgin olive oil

juice of 1 lime

4 radishes, thinly sliced

1 shallot, thinly sliced

2 tbsp chopped fresh cilantro

Celtic sea salt or kosher salt

freshly ground black pepper

Directions:

Put the whisk eggs in a shallow bowl, and the bread crumbs in a second shallow bowl. Sprinkle the fish with flour and season it with pepper and salt. Dredge the fillets in the egg, remove, and coat with the bread crumbs. Spritz the coated fillets with cooking spray. In a large bowl, toss the potato planks with the olive oil. Place the potatoes in your air fryer's basket and top with the breaded fish. Fry at 375°F for 15 minutes, turning halfway through the cooking time until the fish is cooked (cut into the thickest part, it will be opaque and flake easily with a fork). In a small size of the bowl, mix the coleslaw mix, olive oil, lime juice, radishes, shallot, and cilantro. Mix well. Season to taste with salt and pepper. Set aside until serving.

Nutrition:

Calories 366

Fat 13g

Protein 29g

Carbs 34g

23. Creamy Air Fryer Salmon

Preparation Time: 5 minutesCooking Time: 10 minutes

Servings: 2

Ingredients:

¾ lb. salmon, cut into six pieces salt to taste

¼ cup plain yogurt 1 tbsp dill, chopped

3 tbsp light sour cream 1 tbsp olive oil

Directions:

Season the salmon with salt and place it in an air fryer. Drizzle the salmon with olive oil. Air-fry salmon at 285°Fahrenheit and cook for 10-minutes. Mix the dill, yogurt, sour cream, and some salt. Place salmon on a serving dish and drizzle with creamy sauce.

Nutrition:

 Calories 289 Total Fat 9.8g

Carbs 8.6

Protein 14.7g

24.   Air-Fried Cod Sticks

Preparation Time: 12 minutes

Cooking Time: 5 minutes

Servings: 5

Ingredients:

2 large eggs, beaten

3 tbsp milk

2 cups breadcrumbs

1 lb. cod fillets

1 cup almond meal

salt and pepper to taste

Directions:

In a bowl, mix egg and milk. In a shallow dish, combine breadcrumbs, pepper, and salt. In another dish, add the almond meal. Roll the cod sticks into almond meal, dip in egg, and coat in breadcrumbs. Place the coated cod sticks in the air fryer basket. Air fry at 350°Fahrenheit for 12-minutes and

shake the basket halfway through cook time. Serve hot.

Nutrition:

Calories 298

Fat 10.2g,

Carbs 9.5g,

Protein 14.8g

CHAPTER 5

Poultry

25. Fruity Chicken Breasts with BBQ Sauce

Preparation Time: 5 minutes

Cooking Time: 20 minutes

Servings: 2

Ingredients:

2 chicken breasts, cubed

2 green bell peppers, sliced ½ onion, sliced

1 can drain pineapple chunks ½ cup barbecue sauce

Directions

Preheat air fryer on Bake function to 370 F. Thread the green

bell peppers, chicken cubes, onions, and pineapple chunks on the skewers. Brush with barbecue sauce and cook in your air

fryer for 20 minutes until slightly crispy. Serve.

Nutrition:

Calories 296

Fat 10g;

Carbohydrates 5 g;

Protein 34 g;

26.   Savory Honey & Garlic Chicken

Preparation Time: 35 minutes

Cooking Time: 20 minutes

Servings: 4

Ingredients:

2 chicken drumsticks, skin removed

2 tbsp olive oil

2 tbsp honey

½ tbsp garlic, minced

Directions

Add garlic, olive oil, and honey to a sealable zip bag. Add chicken and toss to coat; set aside for 30 minutes. Add the coated chicken to the basket and fit in the baking sheet; cook for 15 minutes at 400 F on Air Fry function, flipping once. Serve and enjoy!

Nutrition: Calories 364; Fat 8 g; Carbohydrates 5g;

Protein 32 g;

27. Faire-Worthy Turkey Legs

Preparation Time: 5 minutes

Cooking Time: 10 minutes Servings: 4

Ingredients:

I turkey leg

1 teaspoon olive oil

1 teaspoon poultry seasoning

1 teaspoon garlic powder

salt and black pepper to taste

Directions:

Warm up the air fryer to 350°F for about 4 minutes.

Coat the leg with the olive oil. Just use your hands and rub it

in.In a small bowl, mix the poultry seasoning, garlic powder,

salt and pepper. Rub it on the turkey leg.Coat the inside of

the air fryer basket with nonstick spray and place the turkey

leg in.Cook for 27 minutes, turning at 14 minutes. Be sure

the leg is done by inserting a meat thermometer in the fleshy

part of the leg and it should read 165 degrees F.

Nutrition:

Calories: 325

Carbohydrates: 8.3g

Fat: 10g

Protein: 18g

CHAPTER 6

Meat

28.   Cheesy Ground Beef 'n Mac Taco Casserole

Preparation Time: 5 minutes

Cooking Time: 25 minutes

Servings: 5

Ingredients:

1 oz. shredded Cheddar cheese

1 oz. shredded Monterey Jack cheese

2 tbsp. chopped green onions

1/2 (10.75oz.) can condensed tomato soup

½ lb. lean ground beef

1/2 cup crushed tortilla chips

¼ lb. macaroni, cooked according to manufacturer's Instructions

1/4 cup chopped onion

1/4 cup sour cream (optional)

1/2 (1.25 oz.) package taco seasoning mix

1/2 (14.5 oz.) can diced tomatoes

Directions:

Lightly grease the baking pan of the air fryer with cooking spray. Add onion and ground beef. For 10 minutes, cook on 360oF. Halfway through cooking time, stir and crumble ground beef. Add taco seasoning, diced tomatoes, and tomato soup. Mix well. Mix in pasta. Sprinkle crushed tortilla chips. Sprinkle cheese. Cook for 15 minutes at 390oF until tops are lightly browned and cheese is melted. Serve and enjoy.

Nutrition:

Calories 329 Fat 17.0g Protein 28.2g

29.   Cheesy Herbs Burger Patties

Preparation Time: 10 minutes

Cooking Time: 25 minutes Servings: 2

Ingredients:

¼ cup cheddar cheese

½ tsp. dried rosemary, crushed

1 lb. lean ground beef

2 green onions, sliced thinly

2 tbsp. chopped parsley

2 tbsp. ketchup

3 tbsp. Dijon mustard

3 tbsp. dry breadcrumbs

salt and pepper to taste

Directions:

In a mixing bowl, combine all ingredients except for the cheddar cheese. Mix using your hands. Use your hands to make burger patties. At the center of each patty, place a tablespoon of cheese and cover with the meat mixture.

Preheat the air fryer to 3900F. Place the grill pan accessory

and cook the patties for 25 minutes. Flip the patties halfway

through the cooking time.

Nutrition:

Calories 359 Fat 14g Protein 29g

30.   Cheesy Potato Casserole the Amish Way

Cooking Time: 45 minutes

Preparation Time: 15 minutes

Cooking Time: 45minutes

Servings: 6

Ingredients:

2 cups frozen shredded hash brown potatoes, thawed

5 medium eggs, lightly beaten

1 cup shredded Cheddar cheese

½ lb. sliced bacon, diced

1/2 sweet onion, chopped

1/2 cup and 2 tablespoons shredded Swiss cheese

3/4 cup small curd cottage cheese

Directions:

Lightly grease the baking pan of the air fryer with cooking spray. For 10 minutes, cook on 330oF the onion and bacon. Discard excess fat. Meanwhile, in a bowl, whisk well Swiss cheese, cottage cheese, cheddar cheese, eggs, and potatoes. Pour into a pan of cooked bacon and mix well. Cook for another 25 minutes. Let it stand in the air fryer for another 10 minutes. Serve and enjoy.

Nutrition:

Calories 341

Fat 22.8g

Protein 21.7g

31.   Cheesy Sausage 'n Grits Bake From Down South

Preparation Time: 10 minutes

Cooking Time: 30 minutes

Servings: 4

Ingredients:

1/2 cup uncooked grits

¼ lb. ground pork sausage

1-1/2 cups water

2 tbsp. butter, divided

2 tbsp. milk

3 eggs

3/4 cup shredded Cheddar cheese, divided

salt and pepper to taste

Directions:

In a large saucepan bring water to a boil. Stir in grits and simmer until liquid is absorbed, around 5 minutes. Stir in ¼ cup cheese and 1 tbsp. butter. Mix well until thoroughly incorporated. Lightly grease the baking pan of the air fryer with cooking spray. Add pork sausage and for 5 minutes, cook on 360oF. Crumble sausage and discard excess fat. Transfer grits into a pan of sausage. In a bowl whisk well, milk and eggs and pour into the pan. Mix well. Dot the top with butter and sprinkle cheese. Season with pepper and salt.

Cook until tops are browned, around 20 minutes. Serve and enjoy.

Nutrition:

Calories 401

Fat 29.9g

Protein 16.5g

32.   Beef Recipe Texas-Rodeo Style

Preparation Time: 20 minutes

Cooking Time:1 hour

Servings: 6

Ingredients:

½ cup honey

½ cup ketchup

½ tsp. dry mustard

1 clove of garlic, minced

1 tbsp. chili powder

2 onion, chopped

3 lb. beef steak sliced

salt and pepper to taste

Directions:

Place all ingredients in a Ziploc bag and allow to marinate in

the fridge for at least 2 hours. Preheat the air fryer to 3900F.

Place the grill pan accessory in the air fryer. Grill the beef for

15 minutes per batch making sure that you flip it every 8 minutes for even grilling. Meanwhile, pour the marinade on a saucepan and allow to simmer over medium heat until the sauce thickens. Baste the beef with the sauce before serving.

Nutrition:

Calories 542

Fat 22g

Protein 37g

CHAPTER 7

Vegetables

33.   Baked Garlic Parsley Potatoes

Preparation TIme: 15 minutes

Cooking Time: 40 minutes Servings: 3

Ingredients:

3 baking potatoes, washed

Parsley for garnishing

1 tablespoon olive oil Sea salt to taste

2 garlic cloves, crushed

Directions:

Preparing the potatoes: make holes using a fork in them.

Season potatoes with salt and cover with garlic puree and

olive oil. Layer the potatoes in the air fryer basket and cook at 390°Fahrenheit and cook for 40-minutes.

Nutrition:

Calories 233 Fat 5.6g Protein 7.8g

34.   Roasted Vegetables

Preparation: 10 minutes Cooking: 30 minutes Servings: 4

Ingredients:

2 cups yellow squash, sliced ½ tsp. salt

½ tsp.pepper 1 tsp. thyme leaves

1 tbsp.oregano, chopped 2 tbsp.s olive oil

1 cup carrots, sliced

Directions:

In a bowl, add zucchini, squash, and carrots. Add oregano, oil, and thyme. Season with pepper and salt. Toss well. Place vegetables in an air fryer basket and cook for 400°Fahrenheit for 30-minutes.

Nutrition:

Calories 264

Fat 12.5g

Protein 7.5g

35. Broccoli Salad

Preparation Time: 5 minutes

Cooking Time: 8minutes

Servings: 4

Ingredients:

1 head broccoli florets separated

1 tbsp. peanut oil

6 cloves garlic, minced

1 tbsp. Chinese rice wine vinegar

salt and black pepper to taste

Directions:

In a bowl, mix broccoli with half of the oil, salt, and pepper and toss. Cook in the air fryer at 350F for 8 minutes. Shake once. Transfer broccoli to a bowl. Add the rest of the peanut oil, rice vinegar, and garlic, and toss well. Serve.

Nutrition: Calories 121 Fat 3g Protein 4g

36.   Brussels Sprouts and Tomatoes Mix

Preparation Time: 5 minutes

Cooking Time: 10 minutes

Servings: 4

Ingredients:

1 lb. brussels sprouts trimmed

salt and black pepper to taste

8 halved cherry tomatoes

¼ cup Green onions chopped

1 tbsp. olive oil

Directions:

Season Brussels sprouts with salt and pepper. Cook in the air fryer at 350F for 10 minutes. Transfer to a bowl. Add olive oil, green onions, cherry tomatoes, salt, and pepper. Toss and serve.

Nutrition: Calories 121 Fat 4g Protein 4g

37. Spicy Chickpeas

Preparation Time: 5 minutes

Cooking Time: 20 minutes Servings: 4

Ingredients:

Olive oil

½ teaspoon ground cumin

½ teaspoon chili powder

¼ teaspoon cayenne pepper

¼ teaspoon salt

1 (19-ounce) can chickpeas, drained and rinsed

Spray a fryer basket lightly with olive oil.

In a bowl, combine the chili powder, cumin, cayenne pepper, and salt.

In a medium bowl, add the chickpeas and lightly spray them with olive oil. Add the spice mixture and toss until coated evenly.

Transfer the chickpeas to the fryer basket. Air fry until the chickpeas reach your desired level of crunchiness, 15 to 20 minutes, making sure to shake the basket every 5 minutes.

Air Fry Like a Pro: I find 20 minutes to be the sweet spot for very crunchy chickpeas. If you prefer them less crispy, cook for about 15 minutes.

These make a great vehicle for experimenting with different seasoning mixes such as Chinese 5-spice, a mixture of curry and turmeric, or herbs de Provence.

Nutrition:

Calories: 122;

Total Fat: 1g;

Saturated Fat: 0g;

Carbohydrates: 22g;

Protein: 6g;

Fiber: 6g;

Sodium: 152mg

CHAPTER 8

Soup and Stews

38. Noodle Soup with Tofu

Preparation: 10 minutes Cooking: 20 minutes Servings: 5

Ingredients:

2 tsp. sesame oil

1 clove garlic, minced

1/2 tsp. Chinese five-spice

1/4 cup scallions, chopped

1 cup hot water

1/2 tsp. chicken base

1 1/2 oz. instant rice noodles

1 cup sugar snap peas

1 cup bean sprouts

1/2 cup tofu cubes

Directions:

Set the Air fryer oven to 375 degrees F for 5 minutes.

Sauté garlic and Chinese five-spice in oil for 1 minute. Add water and chicken base at "Broil" and "More." Add the rice noodles with pot off.

Add last 3 ingredients to a bowl.

Pour the broth over. Insert the cooking tray in the oven. Remove from the Oven when Cooking Time is complete. Put the olive oil in a wok and add the garlic, ginger, and onions. Sauté for about 3 minutes and add carrot mixture, vegetable stock, and Worcestershire sauce.

Serve with scallions and Sriracha sauce.

Nutrition:

Calories 148 Protein 4.6g Carbohydrates 4g

Fat 24.6g

CHAPTER 9

Snacks

39.   Air Fryer Dark Chocolate Ganache

Preparation Time: 1 minute

Cooking Time: 2 minutes

Servings:4

Ingredients:

150 g Dark Chocolate

30 g Butter

4 tbsps. Greek Yoghurt 1 teaspoon Honey

Directions:

Break up dark chocolate into squares.

Place butter, honey and dark chocolate into cake pan and place pan in air fryer basket.

Cook for 2 minutes at320f.

Stir and add in your Greek Yoghurt.

Nutrition:

Calories 295 Carbs 19g

Protein 4g Fat 22g

Saturated Fat 13g

Cholesterol 18mg

Sodium 67mg

Potassium 268mg

Fiber 4g

40. Air Fryer British Victoria Sponge

Preparation Time: 15 minutes

Cooking Time:28 minutes

Servings:8

Ingredients:

100 g Plain Flour

100 g Butter

100 g Caster Sugar

2 Medium Eggs

Cake Filling:

2 tbsps. Strawberry Jam

50 g Butter

100 g Icing Sugar

1 tablespoon Whipped Cream

Directions:

Preheat air fryer to 180c.

Grease a baking dish that can fit into Air fryer

Cream the butter and sugar until they are light and fluffy, beat in the eggs and add a little flour with each of them the gently fold in the remainder of the flour.

Place the mixture into the tin and cook in the Air fryer for 15 minutes on 180C and then on 170C for 10 minutes.

Leave to cool and slice in the middle equally

Cream butter while gradually add the icing sugar and whipped cream until you have a thick and creamy mixture.

Add a layer of strawberry jam and then a layer of cake filling and then add your other sponge on top.

Enjoy!

Nutrition:

Calories 307kcal Carbs 38g

Protein 2g

Fat 16g

Saturated Fat 10g

41.   Sriracha Broccoli

Preparation Time: 10 minutes

Cooking Time:6 minutes Servings:5

Ingredients:

1 teaspoon sriracha

1 tablespoon olive oil

1 teaspoon flax seeds

1 teaspoon ground white pepper

1 teaspoon kosher salt

1-pound broccoli

4 tablespoons chicken stock

Directions:

Wash the broccoli and separate it into the florets.

Then combine the chicken stock, ground white pepper, flax seeds, and sriracha. Add the olive oil and whisk the mixture.

Preheat the air fryer to 400 F. Put the broccoli florets in the air fryer basket rack and sprinkle the vegetables with the sriracha mixture, Cook the broccoli for 6 minutes.

When the time is over – shake the broccoli gently and transfer it to the serving plates.

Enjoy!

Nutrition:

Calories 61

Fat 33,

Fiber 1.4

Carbs 4.5

Protein 9.5

42. Cheddar Cheese Sliced Cauliflower

Preparation Time: 15 minutes

Cooking Time:11 minutes

Servings:7

Ingredients:

14 oz. cauliflower

6 oz. Cheddar cheese, sliced

1 teaspoon salt

1 teaspoon ground black pepper

1 teaspoon butter, frozen

1 teaspoon dried dill

1 tablespoon olive oil

Directions:

Wash the cauliflower head carefully and slice it into the servings. Sprinkle the sliced cauliflower with the salt, ground black pepper, and dried dill.

Grate the frozen butter. Then sprinkle the cauliflower with the olive oil from the both sides.

Preheat the air fryer to 400 F.

Place the cauliflower slices in the air fryer rack and cook it for 7 minutes. After this, turn the cauliflower slices into another side and sprinkle them with the grated frozen butter. Cook the cauliflower for 3 minutes more.

Then place the cheese slices over the cauliflower and cook it for 1 minute more.

Transfer the cooked cauliflower to the serving plates with the help of the spatula.

Serve the dish immediately.

Enjoy!

Nutrition:

Calories 135, Fat 13,

Fiber 0.4, Carbs 1.5, Protein 9.5

43.   Cauliflower Head

Preparation Time: 10 minutes

Cooking Time:15 minutes Servings:6

Ingredients:

1-pound cauliflower head

1 teaspoon onion powder

½ cup heavy cream

5 oz. Parmesan, shredded

1 teaspoon garlic powder

1 teaspoon salt

Directions:

Combine the heavy cream, onion powder, garlic powder, salt, and shredded Parmesan cheese in the big bowl. Mix the mixture up.

Then place the cauliflower head in the heavy cream mixture.

Coat the cauliflower with the heavy cream mixture using the hands. Then preheat the air fryer to 360 F.

Put the cauliflower head in the air fryer basket and cook it for 12 minutes. After this, increase the temperature to 390 F and cook the cauliflower head for 3 minutes. When the time is over, and the cauliflower is cooked – serve it immediately.

Enjoy!

Nutrition:

Calories 132,

Fat 13,

Fiber 0.4,

Carbs 1.5,

Protein 9.5

CHAPTER 10

Desserts

44. Cream Cheese Muffins

Preparation Time: 10 minutes

Cooking Time: 16 minutes Servings: 10

Ingredients:

2 eggs

1/2 cup erythritol

8 oz cream cheese

1 tsp ground cinnamon

1/2 tsp vanilla

Directions:

Preheat the air fryer to 325 F. In a bowl, mix together cream cheese, vanilla, erythritol, and eggs until soft. Pour batter into the silicone muffin molds and sprinkle cinnamon on top. Place muffin molds into the air fryer basket and cook for 16 minutes. Serve and enjoy.

Nutrition:

Calories 90

Fat 8.8 g

Protein 2.8 g

45. Cinnamon Apple Chips

Preparation Time: 10 minutes

Cooking Time: 8 minutes

Servings: 6

Ingredients:

3 Granny Smith apples, wash, core and thinly slice

1 tsp ground cinnamon

Pinch of salt

Directions:

Rub apple slices with cinnamon and salt and place into the air fryer basket. Cook at 390 F for 8 minutes. Turn halfway through. Serve and enjoy.

Nutrition:

Calories 41

Fat 0 g Carbohydrates 11 g

Sugar 8 g

Protein 0 g

46.   Choco Mug Cake

Preparation: 5 minutesCooking: 20 minutes Servings: 1

Ingredients:

1 egg, lightly beaten 1 tbsp heavy cream

¼ tsp baking powder 2 tbsp unsweetened cocoa powder

2 tbsp Erythritol ½ tsp vanilla

1 tbsp peanut butter 1 tsp salt

Directions:

Preheat the air fryer to 400 F. In a bowl, mix together all ingredients until well combined. Spray mug with cooking spray. Pour batter in mug and place in the air fryer and cook for 20 minutes. Serve and enjoy.

Nutrition:

Calories 241 Fat 19 g

Carbohydrates 10 g Sugar 2 g

Protein 12 g

Cholesterol 184 mg

47. Almond Bars

Preparation Time: 10 minutes

Cooking Time: 35 minutes Servings: 12

Ingredients:

2 eggs, lightly beaten

1 cup erythritol

½ tsp vanilla

¼ cup water

½ cup butter, softened

¾ cup cherries, pitted

1 ½ cup almond flour

1 tbsp xanthan gum

½ tsp salt

Directions:

In a bowl, mix together almond flour, erythritol, eggs, vanilla, butter, and salt until dough formed. Press dough in air fryer baking dish.

Place in the air fryer and cook at 375 F for 10 minutes. Meanwhile, mix together cherries, xanthan gum, and water. Pour cherry mixture over cooked dough and cook for 25 minutes more. Slice and serve.

Nutrition:

Calories 168

Fat 15 g

Carbohydrates 5 g

Protein 4 g

48.   Coconut Berry Pudding

Preparation Time: 10 minutes

Cooking Time: 15 minutes Servings: 6

Ingredients:

2 cups coconut cream

1 lime zest, grated

3 tbsp erythritol

¼ cup blueberries

1/3 cup blackberries

Directions:

Add all ingredients into the blender and blend until well combined. Spray 6 ramekins with cooking spray. Pour blended mixture into the ramekins and place in the air fryer. Cook at 340 F for 15 minutes. Serve and enjoy.

Nutrition:

Calories 190 Fat 19 g Carbohydrates 6 g Sugar 3.7 g

Protein 2 g

49.   Coffee Cookies

Preparation Time: 10 minutes

Cooking Time: 15 minutes

Servings: 12

Ingredients:

1-cup almond flour

2 eggs, lightly beaten

2 tsp baking powder

½ tbsp cinnamon

¼-cup erythritol

¼ cup brewed espresso

½ cup ghee, melted

Directions:

Add all ingredients into the bowl and mix until well combined. Place cookie sheet into the air fryer basket. Make small cookies from mixture and place into the air fryer basket on cookie sheet. Cook at 350 F for 15 minutes. Serve and enjoy.

Nutrition:

Calories 141

Fat 14 g

Carbohydrates 2.8 g

Sugar 0.4 g

Protein 3 g

50.   Marble Cheesecake

Preparation Time: 10 minutes

Cooking Time 20 minutes

Servings: 8

Ingredients

1-cup graham cracker crumbs

3 tablespoons butter, at room temperature

1 ½ (8-ounce) packages cream cheese, at room temperature

⅓ Cup sugar

2 eggs, beaten

1-tablespoon all-purpose flour

1-teaspoon vanilla extract

¼ cup chocolate syrup

Directions:

In a small bowl, stir together the graham cracker crumbs and

butter.

Press the crust into the bottom of a 6-by-2-inch round baking pan and freeze to set while you prepare the filling.

In a medium bowl, stir together the cream cheese and sugar until mixed well. One at a time, beat in the eggs. Add the flour and vanilla and stir to combine. Transfer ⅔ cup of filling to a small bowl and stir in the chocolate syrup until combined.

Insert the crisper plate into the basket and the basket into the unit. Preheat the unit by selecting BAKE, setting the temperature to 325°F, and setting the time to 3 minutes. Select START/STOP to begin.

Pour the vanilla filling into the pan with the crust. Drop the chocolate filling over the vanilla filling by the spoonful. With a clean butter knife, stir the fillings in a zigzag pattern to marbleize them. Do not let the knife touch the crust. Once the unit is preheated, place the pan into the basket.

Select BAKE, set the temperature to 325°F, and set the time to 20 minutes. Select START/STOP to begin. When the cooking is done, the cheesecake should be just set. Cool on a wire rack for 1 hour. Refrigerate the cheesecake until firm before slicing.

Nutrition:

Calories 311

Fat 21g

Carbohydrates: 25g

Protein6g

Conclusion

Unlike frying things in a typical pan on gas which fails to make your fries crisp and leaves your samosa uncooked due to uneven heat. The inbuilt kitchen deep fryers do it all; you can have perfectly crisp French fries like the one you get in restaurants. Your samosas will be perfectly cooked inside- out. Well, the list doesn't end here it goes on and on the potato wedges, chicken and much more. You can make many starters and dishes using fryer and relish the taste buds of your loved ones.

The new air fryers come along with a lot of features, so you don't mess up doing things enjoy your cooking experience. The free hot to set the temperature according to your convenience both mechanically and electronically. Oil filters to reuse the oil and use it for a long run. With the ventilation system to reduce and eliminate the frying odor. In a few models you also get the automatic timers and alarm set for convenient cooking, frying I mean. Also, the auto- push and raise feature to immerse or hold back the frying basket to achieve the perfect frying aim. So, why should you wait? I am sure you don't want to mess in your kitchen when grilling, baking of frying your food, right? Get yourself an air fryer. Thank you for purchasing this cookbook I hope you will apply all the acquired knowledge productively.

CPSIA information can be obtained
at www.ICGtesting.com
Printed in the USA
BVHW091017190421
605287BV00002B/193

9 781801 658539